Vietnamese Coffee Recipes

Exploring the Rich and Aromatic World of Authentic Vietnamese Coffee Creations

VIETNAMESE COFFEE RECIPES

First edition. November 6, 2023.

ISBN: 979-8223857655

Written by john ahmad.

John Ahmad

Chapter Outline:

Introduction to Vietnamese Coffee Culture

- The Historical Significance of Coffee in Vietnam
- Coffee as a Social and Culinary Tradition
- A Glimpse into the Different Coffee Styles

Essential Tools and Ingredients

- Must-Have Coffee Brewing Equipment
- Types of Vietnamese Coffee Beans
- Navigating Sweeteners and Additions

Traditional Vietnamese Coffee (Cà Phê Sữa Đá)

- Brewing the Perfect Cup of Strong Drip Coffee
- Balancing Coffee with Sweetened Condensed Milk
- Serving over Ice: Tips for Refreshing Enjoyment

Creamy Egg Coffee (Cà Phê Trứng)

- Whipping Up the Iconic Egg Coffee Froth
- Achieving the Ideal Sweetness and Texture
- Variations: Egg Cream Coffee and More

Iced Coconut Coffee (Cà Phê Dừa)

- Infusing Coffee with Rich Coconut Flavor
- Blending and Chilling Techniques
- Garnishing and Serving Suggestions

Condensed Milk Coffee Popsicles

- Turning Vietnamese Coffee into Frozen Delights

Chapter 2: Essential Tools and Ingredients

To embark on a journey through the world of Vietnamese coffee, it's essential to equip yourself with the right tools and ingredients. From the brewing equipment that brings out the nuances of each bean to the coffee types that form the foundation of your creations, and the sweeteners and additions that add depth to your drinks, this chapter lays the groundwork for your coffee exploration.

Must-Have Coffee Brewing Equipment

Traditional Drip Filter: The heart of Vietnamese coffee brewing, the drip filter, or "phin," is a small metal device that allows you to extract the full flavor of coffee. It consists of a perforated compartment for coffee grounds and a chamber for hot water to drip through. Its slow and meticulous extraction process contributes to the distinct character of Vietnamese coffee.

French Press: While not traditional to Vietnamese coffee, a French press can be a versatile tool for brewing a richer cup. Its immersion method extracts more of the coffee's oils and flavors, offering a different dimension to your coffee experience.

Coffee Grinder: Invest in a burr grinder to ensure consistency in grind size. This is crucial for achieving the right extraction and maintaining the integrity of the coffee's flavor.

Scale and Timer: Precise measurements and timing are key to consistent brewing. A digital scale and timer help you achieve the perfect coffee-to-water ratio and extraction time.

Types of Vietnamese Coffee Beans

Robusta: The backbone of Vietnamese coffee, robusta beans thrive in the country's central highlands. Known for their bold and earthy flavor, as well as high caffeine content, robusta beans are the foundation of many traditional Vietnamese coffee drinks.

Arabica: While not as common as robusta, arabica beans are gaining popularity in Vietnam. They bring a smoother and more nuanced flavor profile to your coffee creations, often with notes of fruit and florals.

Blends: Many Vietnamese coffees are blends of different bean varieties, carefully curated to achieve a specific taste. Experimenting with various blends can lead to exciting new flavors.

Navigating Sweeteners and Additions

Sweetened Condensed Milk: A staple in Vietnamese coffee culture, sweetened condensed milk adds a rich and indulgent sweetness to your brews. It's an integral component of Cà Phê Sữa Đá and other coffee drinks.

Coconut Milk: For a tropical twist, consider using coconut milk as a dairy alternative. It adds a creamy texture and a hint of coconut flavor to your coffee.

Egg Yolks: An essential element in Egg Coffee (Cà Phê Trứng), egg yolks create a velvety foam that adds a unique creaminess to your coffee.

Sugar and Syrups: Whether it's traditional granulated sugar, flavored syrups, or natural sweeteners like honey, these additions can customize the sweetness of your drinks to your preference.

Equipped with these tools and armed with an understanding of the different coffee beans and sweeteners, you're ready to dive into the recipes that await you. With each creation, you'll have the chance to explore the interplay of flavors, experiment with ingredients, and craft a cup of Vietnamese coffee that's uniquely yours.

Chapter 3: Traditional Vietnamese Coffee (Cà Phê Sữa Đá)

Delving into the heart of Vietnamese coffee culture, we explore the iconic Cà Phê Sữa Đá, a time-honored concoction that epitomizes the harmonious blend of strong coffee and velvety sweetness. In this chapter, we'll uncover the art of brewing the perfect cup of drip coffee, striking the delicate balance between the robust coffee flavors and the luscious touch of sweetened condensed milk. And as the final touch, we'll guide you through the art of serving this delightfully refreshing beverage over ice.

Brewing the Perfect Cup of Strong Drip Coffee

Choose Your Coffee Beans: Begin with high-quality Vietnamese robusta beans for an authentic flavor. If you prefer a milder taste, consider blending robusta with arabica beans.

Grind to Perfection: Grind the coffee beans to a medium-coarse consistency. The right grind ensures optimal extraction and a well-rounded flavor profile.

Assemble the Drip Filter: Place the drip filter over a sturdy glass or cup. Add about 2-3 tablespoons of coffee grounds to the filter.

Pre-Wet the Coffee: Pour a small amount of hot water (about 1-2 tablespoons) over the coffee grounds to saturate them. Allow the coffee to bloom for about 20-30 seconds.

Drip Brewing: Slowly pour hot water (just off the boil) into the drip filter until it's nearly full. Place the filter's lid on top and allow the coffee to drip through. This gradual extraction method yields a strong and full-bodied brew.

Patience is Key: Drip brewing takes time – usually around 5-6 minutes. The slower extraction results in a coffee that's rich and nuanced in flavor.

Balancing Coffee with Sweetened Condensed Milk

Measure the Milk: In a separate glass, measure 2-3 tablespoons of sweetened condensed milk. Adjust the amount based on your desired level of sweetness.

Mixing Magic: Once your coffee is fully brewed, give it a good stir to combine the flavors and dissolve any remaining condensed milk at the bottom of the glass.

Gradual Incorporation: Begin by pouring a small amount of brewed coffee into the glass with the condensed milk. Stir vigorously to create a smooth mixture.

The Final Blend: Gradually pour the rest of the coffee into the glass, continuing to stir as you pour. The result is a velvety blend where the coffee's boldness intertwines seamlessly with the condensed milk's sweetness.

Serving over Ice: Tips for Refreshing Enjoyment

Prepare a Glass of Ice: Fill a tall glass with ice cubes. This will be the foundation for your Cà Phê Sữa Đá.

Pour and Chill: Gently pour your brewed coffee and condensed milk mixture over the ice. The contrast between the hot coffee and the cold ice creates a delightful sensory experience.

Stir and Sip: Give the drink a final stir to ensure a consistent flavor. As you sip, you'll experience a symphony of flavors that evolve as the ice melts and melds with the coffee.

Garnish and Enjoy: For an extra touch of indulgence, consider topping your Cà Phê Sữa Đá with a dollop of whipped cream or a drizzle of chocolate syrup. Enjoy your creation slowly, savoring the layers of taste and the cool relief it brings.

With the knowledge of brewing a perfect cup of strong drip coffee, the art of balancing its flavors with sweetened condensed milk, and the refreshing presentation over ice, you're now equipped to create your own Cà Phê Sữa Đá – a beloved classic that captures the essence of Vietnamese coffee culture.

Chapter 4: Creamy Egg Coffee (Cà Phê Trứng)

In this chapter, we embark on a journey to uncover the exquisite indulgence of Cà Phê Trứng, or Egg Coffee. A beloved Vietnamese creation, this unique concoction combines the richness of egg yolks with the robustness of coffee to create a velvety foam that transforms your coffee ritual into a decadent dessert-like experience. We'll guide you through the art of whipping up the iconic egg coffee froth, achieving the perfect balance of sweetness and texture, and even explore delightful variations like Egg Cream Coffee.

Whipping Up the Iconic Egg Coffee Froth

Separate the Eggs: Begin by separating egg yolks from the whites. You'll only need the yolks for this recipe.

Whisk with Sugar: In a mixing bowl, combine egg yolks and a tablespoon of sugar. Whisk vigorously until the mixture becomes pale and frothy. This step is crucial for achieving the desired creamy texture.

Coffee Base: Brew a strong cup of Vietnamese coffee using your preferred method. Let it cool slightly before moving on to the next step.

Incorporating the Froth: Gradually add a portion of the egg yolk mixture to the cup of coffee. Gently whisk or stir to blend the froth with the coffee. This creates the distinct velvety layer that defines Egg Coffee.

Achieving the Ideal Sweetness and Texture

Customizing Sweetness: The level of sweetness is customizable to your taste. Adjust the amount of sugar in the egg yolk mixture to achieve the desired balance between the coffee's bitterness and the sweetness of the froth.

Creamy Consistency: The key to achieving the perfect texture lies in the whisking process. Whisk the egg yolks and sugar until the mixture is light and fluffy. This will result in a creamy foam that sits beautifully atop your coffee.

Temperature Matters: It's essential to work with slightly cooled coffee. If the coffee is too hot, it might cook the egg yolks, altering the desired texture.

Variations: Egg Cream Coffee and More

Egg Cream Coffee: A lighter variation of Egg Coffee, this version omits the coffee base. Instead, the whipped egg yolks are combined with milk or cream and served as a dessert-like beverage on their own. It's a delightful option for those who want to savor the essence of Egg Coffee without the coffee itself.

Egg Coffee Latté: Elevate your Egg Coffee experience by creating a latté. Brew a strong shot of espresso and top it with the frothy egg mixture. The espresso's intensity adds depth to the overall flavor profile.

Chocolate Infusion: For a decadent twist, consider adding a touch of melted chocolate to the egg yolk mixture. The marriage of chocolate, coffee, and creamy foam creates a sensory symphony that's sure to delight.

Elevating Your Coffee Ritual

With the mastery of whipping up the iconic egg coffee froth, achieving the perfect sweetness and texture, and exploring delightful variations, you're poised to elevate your coffee ritual to new heights. Cà Phê Trứng isn't just a beverage; it's a testament to the creativity and artistry that define Vietnamese coffee culture. As you indulge in this unique concoction, you'll experience the harmonious blend of flavors that has captured the hearts of coffee enthusiasts around the world.

Chapter 5: Iced Coconut Coffee (Cà Phê Dừa)

Prepare to embark on a tropical journey with Cà Phê Dừa, or Iced Coconut Coffee. This delightful creation infuses the bold flavors of coffee with the rich and creamy essence of coconut, resulting in a refreshing and indulgent beverage that's perfect for sipping on a hot day. In this chapter, we'll guide you through the art of infusing coffee with coconut flavor, blending and chilling techniques to achieve the ideal consistency, and garnishing and serving suggestions to elevate your Iced Coconut Coffee experience.

Infusing Coffee with Rich Coconut Flavor

Select Quality Ingredients: The foundation of a great Iced Coconut Coffee is premium-quality Vietnamese robusta coffee beans. Their robust and full-bodied flavor pairs harmoniously with the rich creaminess of coconut.

Coconut Milk or Cream: You have a choice between using full-fat coconut milk for a silky texture or opting for the even richer consistency of coconut cream. Whichever you choose, the coconut's natural sweetness will meld with the coffee's bitterness to create a delightful balance.

Coconut Essence or Extract: To intensify the coconut aroma, consider adding a few drops of coconut essence or extract to the brewed coffee while it's still warm. This subtle addition will enhance the overall coconut experience.

Infusion Process: Brew a strong cup of Vietnamese coffee using your preferred method. As the coffee steeps, gently stir in a few tablespoons of coconut milk or cream and a drop or two of coconut essence. The warmth of the coffee will coax out the flavors and allow them to meld into a harmonious symphony.

Blending and Chilling Techniques

Blending for Creaminess: After your infused coffee has cooled to room temperature, it's time to embark on the blending process. Transfer the coffee to a blender, and add a generous amount of ice along with an additional splash of coconut milk or cream. The ice will not only chill the mixture but also contribute to its lusciously creamy consistency.

Achieving the Ideal Consistency: Blend the concoction until it reaches a luxurious, velvety texture. The ice should be fully incorporated, resulting in a drink that's refreshingly cold and exceptionally smooth.

Adjusting Thickness: Should you find the blended coffee to be thicker than desired, consider adding a touch of cold brewed coffee or a bit more coconut milk. This step ensures that you achieve the perfect balance of flavors and thickness.

Chilling: Transfer the blended mixture to a tall glass filled with ice. As you pour the mixture over the ice, you'll be treated to a tantalizing dance of steam and cold, the hallmark of a perfectly chilled beverage.

Garnishing and Serving Suggestions

Coconut Shavings: Elevate your Iced Coconut Coffee's presentation and texture by sprinkling a handful of toasted coconut shavings on top. The delicate crunch of the shavings complements the creamy drink, while their aroma adds to the overall sensory experience.

Whipped Cream: For those seeking an extra layer of indulgence, a generous dollop of whipped cream atop your Iced Coconut Coffee will do the trick. The creaminess of the whipped topping plays harmoniously with the coffee and coconut, creating a symphony of flavors.

Caramel Drizzle: Delight your taste buds with a drizzle of caramel syrup over the whipped cream. The interplay of caramel's sweetness, the rich coconut, and the coffee's boldness will take your Iced Coconut Coffee to new heights of flavor complexity.

Serve with a Straw: To fully appreciate the intermingling of flavors, it's best to enjoy your Iced Coconut Coffee through a straw. Each sip allows you to experience the layers of coconut, coffee, and creaminess in perfect harmony.

A Tropical Escape in Every Sip

With the knowledge of infusing coffee with rich coconut flavor, mastering the blending and chilling techniques, and elevating your Iced Coconut Coffee with garnishes and presentation, you're ready to transport yourself to a tropical paradise with every sip. Cà Phê Dừa captures the essence of Vietnam's lush landscapes and the vibrant spirit of its coffee culture. So sit back, relax, and indulge in the cooling delight of Iced Coconut Coffee – a true tropical escape in a glass.

Chapter 6: Condensed Milk Coffee Popsicles

In this chapter, we're diving into the world of frozen delights with Condensed Milk Coffee Popsicles. Taking the beloved flavors of Vietnamese coffee and transforming them into a refreshing and indulgent treat, these popsicles are a delightful way to experience coffee in a new and exciting form. Learn how to create these frozen wonders, discover the right popsicle molds and freezing tips, and explore creative flavor combinations that will have you savoring coffee in a whole new way.

Turning Vietnamese Coffee into Frozen Delights

Choosing the Right Coffee: Just as you would for traditional Vietnamese coffee, select high-quality robusta beans for a rich and bold coffee base. Consider adjusting the coffee concentration slightly to accommodate the freezing process.

Sweetened Condensed Milk: A quintessential ingredient in Vietnamese coffee, sweetened condensed milk plays a central role in these popsicles. It adds creaminess, sweetness, and a touch of nostalgia to every bite.

Infusing the Coffee: Brew a strong cup of Vietnamese coffee and allow it to cool to room temperature. Stir in sweetened condensed milk to your desired level of sweetness, keeping in mind that freezing can dull flavors slightly.

Popsicle Molds and Freezing Tips

Choosing the Right Molds: Opt for popsicle molds that suit your preference – whether it's classic popsicle shapes, fun designs, or even reusable silicone molds. The molds you choose will influence the overall presentation of your popsicles.

Layering Technique: To achieve a visually appealing popsicle, consider a layered approach. Pour a small amount of the coffee mixture into the mold, followed by a layer of sweetened condensed milk. Continue alternating layers until the molds are filled.

Inserting Sticks: Once you've layered the popsicle mixture, insert popsicle sticks into each mold. The sticks should stand upright without sinking too deeply into the mixture.

Freezing Time: Freeze the popsicles for several hours or until they're completely solid. The exact freezing time can vary depending on your freezer's temperature and the size of the popsicles.

Creative Flavor Combinations

Mocha Swirl: Incorporate chocolate into your popsicles by drizzling chocolate syrup between the layers. The interplay of coffee, condensed milk, and chocolate creates a delightful mocha experience.

Coconut Coffee Fusion: Take inspiration from the classic Iced Coconut Coffee and infuse your popsicles with the essence of coconut. Add a layer of coconut milk between the coffee and condensed milk layers for a tropical twist.

Vanilla Coffee Elegance: Enhance the coffee's flavor with a touch of vanilla extract. This addition creates a beautifully balanced popsicle that's both aromatic and refreshing.

Caramel Delight: Elevate your popsicles with a caramel swirl. Add a layer of caramel sauce between the coffee and condensed milk layers for a luscious burst of sweetness.

Savoring Coffee in a New Form

With the knowledge of turning Vietnamese coffee into frozen delights, understanding the nuances of popsicle molds and freezing, and exploring creative flavor combinations, you're well-equipped to savor coffee in an entirely new form. Condensed Milk Coffee Popsicles offer a delightful fusion of tradition and innovation, capturing the essence of Vietnamese coffee culture in a playful and refreshing way. So, beat the heat and indulge in the icy pleasure of these popsicles – a treat that encapsulates the soul of Vietnamese coffee in every lick.

Chapter 7: Coffee and Condensed Milk Flan

Prepare to indulge in a delightful fusion of flavors with Coffee and Condensed Milk Flan. This chapter explores the art of incorporating the bold richness of Vietnamese coffee into the classic flan, resulting in a dessert that's a harmonious blend of coffee intensity and creamy indulgence. Learn how to balance the coffee's robust character, achieve the perfect creaminess, master caramelization techniques, and elevate your presentation to create a show-stopping dessert that captures the essence of both coffee and tradition.

Incorporating Coffee into the Classic Flan

Selecting the Right Coffee: Opt for high-quality Vietnamese robusta beans to capture the essence of Vietnamese coffee. A bold and robust coffee flavor will complement the creaminess of the flan.

Infusion Process: Brew a strong cup of Vietnamese coffee and allow it to cool. This coffee infusion will be the cornerstone of your Coffee and Condensed Milk Flan.

Flan Mixture: Create the flan base by combining sweetened condensed milk, whole milk, and eggs. The combination of these ingredients forms the foundation of your creamy dessert.

Balancing Intensity: When incorporating coffee into the flan mixture, keep in mind that the coffee's intensity will mellow during the baking process. Adjust the amount of coffee infusion to achieve your desired level of coffee flavor.

Balancing Coffee Intensity with Creaminess

Texture and Creaminess: Achieving the perfect flan texture is essential. The custard should be velvety and smooth, with a delicate jiggle when gently shaken.

Cream-to-Coffee Ratio: Strike a balance between the coffee infusion and the creamy flan mixture. Too much coffee can overpower the custard, while too little may not deliver the desired coffee flavor.

Taste Testing: Before baking, taste the flan mixture to ensure that the coffee flavor is well-balanced and harmonious with the creaminess of the custard.

Caramelization and Presentation

Caramelizing the Sugar: To create the signature caramel layer at the bottom of the flan, melt sugar in a saucepan until it transforms into a rich golden-brown syrup. Be cautious, as the process can be quick and requires careful attention.

Coating the Mold: Pour the caramelized sugar into the bottom of each flan mold, swirling to evenly coat the bottom. The caramelization adds depth and sweetness to the dessert.

Pouring the Mixture: Gently pour the flan mixture into the molds over the caramel layer. The mixture will envelop the caramel as it bakes, creating a stunning visual contrast.

Baking and Chilling: Bake the flan in a water bath until set. After baking, allow the flans to cool and chill in the refrigerator for several hours to enhance their flavor and texture.

Unmolding and Serving: To serve, carefully run a knife around the edge of each mold to loosen the flan. Invert the mold onto a serving plate to reveal the luscious caramel layer on top.

A Fusion of Flavor and Tradition

With the knowledge of incorporating coffee into the classic flan, achieving the ideal balance of coffee and creaminess, mastering caramelization techniques, and presenting your Coffee and Condensed Milk Flan with finesse, you're ready to create a dessert that's as impressive in flavor as it is in presentation. This fusion of Vietnamese coffee and timeless flan tradition showcases the versatility of coffee as it transforms into a memorable dessert that's sure to leave a lasting impression on your guests.

Chapter 8: Coffee-Rubbed Grilled Meat

Prepare for a culinary adventure that marries the bold flavors of coffee with the savory satisfaction of grilled meat. In this chapter, we delve into the intricate world of Coffee-Rubbed Grilled Meat, guiding you through the creation of aromatic coffee-based rubs, imparting marination techniques that enhance the meat's tenderness and flavor, providing expert tips on achieving the perfect grill, and offering inspired pairing suggestions that will elevate your dining experience.

Creating Flavorful Coffee-Based Rubs

Coffee Selection: Begin by choosing a Vietnamese coffee that resonates with the type of meat you'll be grilling. A dark roast with robust flavor complements hearty meats, while a medium roast works well with poultry.

Amplifying Complexity: Elevate your rub's profile by adding complementary spices and herbs. Smoked paprika lends a smoky dimension, chili powder brings a hint of heat, cumin adds earthiness, garlic powder contributes depth, and dried herbs provide aromatic notes.

Balancing Sweetness and Savory: Achieve a harmonious balance by incorporating both sweet and savory elements. Brown sugar or honey adds a touch of sweetness, while a judicious amount of salt and freshly ground pepper enhances the savory dimension.

Texture and Crunch: To create an enticing textural experience, consider including crushed nuts or seeds in your rub mixture. They add a delightful crunch that complements the meat's tenderness.

Marinating Techniques for Various Meats

Meat Selection: Coffee-based rubs pair splendidly with a diverse range of meats. For chicken, the rub's boldness can complement its mild flavor, while for beef and pork, the coffee's richness harmonizes beautifully.

Dry Rub Application: Generously coat the meat with the coffee rub mixture, ensuring an even distribution. Gently press the rub into the meat's surface to help it adhere. Allow the rub to sit on the meat for at least an hour, or ideally, refrigerate it overnight for a more profound infusion of flavors.

Wet Marination: Experiment with a wet marinade by combining the coffee rub with oil, citrus juice, or vinegar. This not only imparts flavor but also aids in tenderizing the meat, resulting in a succulent texture

Marination Time: Marinating times differ based on the type of meat and its thickness. Larger cuts like roasts benefit from extended marination, while smaller cuts like chicken breasts require less time. Refer to your recipe or recommended guidelines.

Grilling and Pairing Suggestions

Perfect Grill Setup: Preheat your grill to the appropriate temperature for the meat you're cooking. For coffee-rubbed meats, medium-high heat often works well. The sugars in the rub can caramelize, forming a tantalizing crust.

Grilling Times: Grilling times vary depending on the type of meat and its thickness. Use a meat thermometer to gauge doneness – chicken should reach 165°F (74°C), pork and beef temperatures will vary based on desired doneness.

Pairing with Sides: Accompany your Coffee-Rubbed Grilled Meat with sides that enhance the experience. Roasted vegetables offer earthy balance, tangy slaws provide refreshing contrast, and herbed grains add complexity.

Wine Pairings: The robust flavors of Coffee-Rubbed Grilled Meat can stand up to wines with body and structure. Consider pairing with red wines like Malbec, Zinfandel, or a bold Cabernet Sauvignon for a harmonious match.

Elevating the Grilling Experience

With an understanding of crafting flavorful coffee-based rubs, mastering marination techniques, achieving grill perfection, and exploring inspired pairing suggestions, you're poised to elevate your grilling experience to new heights. Coffee-Rubbed Grilled Meat is an ode to the marriage of robust coffee and savory meat, resulting in creations that tantalize the senses and celebrate the culinary possibilities that arise when tradition meets innovation. Whether for gatherings or everyday indulgence, these coffee-infused dishes will undoubtedly become a memorable and cherished addition to your culinary repertoire.

Chapter 9: Coffee-Marinated Tofu

Venture into the world of plant-based indulgence with Coffee-Marinated Tofu. In this chapter, we explore the innovative union of robust Vietnamese coffee with the versatile canvas of tofu. Discover the art of infusing tofu with coffee essence, achieving a harmonious balance of flavors, and mastering the cooking techniques of pan-frying and baking. This culinary journey promises a delightful blend of textures and tastes that's sure to captivate both coffee enthusiasts and plant-based enthusiasts alike.

Infusing Tofu with Coffee Essence

Tofu Selection: Opt for extra-firm tofu, as its dense texture is better suited to soaking up flavors without falling apart during marination and cooking.

Coffee Concentration: Brew a strong cup of Vietnamese coffee and let it cool to room temperature. The coffee's richness will infuse the tofu with depth and complexity.

Marination Time: Allow the tofu to marinate for at least an hour, or overnight for a more profound coffee infusion. The longer marination time ensures that the flavors penetrate the tofu's interior.

Flavor Accents: Enhance the coffee's profile by incorporating complementary flavors. Ingredients like garlic, soy sauce, and a touch of sweetness (such as maple syrup or brown sugar) work beautifully.

Pan-Fried Coffee-Marinated Tofu

Ingredients:

- 1 block (14 oz / 400g) extra-firm tofu
- 1/4 cup brewed Vietnamese coffee, cooled
- 2 cloves garlic, minced
- 2 tablespoons soy sauce

- 1 tablespoon maple syrup or brown sugar
- 1 tablespoon vegetable oil, for frying
- Salt and pepper, to taste
- Fresh cilantro or green onions, for garnish (optional)

Instructions:

1. Prepare the Tofu: Gently press the tofu to remove excess water. Cut the tofu into slices or cubes, whichever you prefer.

1. Create the Marinade: In a bowl, combine the brewed coffee, minced garlic, soy sauce, and maple syrup (or brown sugar). Season with a pinch of salt and pepper. Mix well to create the marinade.

1. Marinate the Tofu: Place the tofu slices or cubes in a shallow dish or resealable bag. Pour the marinade over the tofu, ensuring each piece is well coated. Cover or seal the container and refrigerate for at least an hour, or ideally overnight.

1. Pan-Fry the Tofu: Heat a non-stick skillet over medium-high heat. Add the vegetable oil and let it heat up. Carefully place the marinated tofu in the skillet, allowing any excess marinade to drip off. Cook until each side is golden brown and crispy, about 3-4 minutes per side.

1. Serve: Once the tofu is cooked to your desired level of crispiness, remove it from the skillet and place it on a serving platter. Garnish with fresh cilantro or green onions, if desired.

1. Enjoy: Serve the Pan-Fried Coffee-Marinated Tofu as a main dish alongside your favorite sides or incorporate it into salads, wraps, or sandwiches for a flavorful plant-based delight.

Baked Coffee-Marinated Tofu
Ingredients:

- 1 block (14 oz / 400g) extra-firm tofu
- 1/4 cup brewed Vietnamese coffee, cooled
- 2 cloves garlic, minced
- 2 tablespoons soy sauce
- 1 tablespoon maple syrup or brown sugar
- Salt and pepper, to taste
- Cooking spray or oil, for greasing
- Fresh cilantro or green onions, for garnish (optional)

Instructions:

1. Prepare the Tofu: Gently press the tofu to remove excess water. Cut the tofu into slices or cubes, as desired.

1. Create the Marinade: In a bowl, combine the brewed coffee, minced garlic, soy sauce, and maple syrup (or brown sugar). Season with a pinch of salt and pepper. Mix well to create the marinade.

1. Marinate the Tofu: Place the tofu slices or cubes in a shallow dish or resealable bag. Pour the marinade over the tofu, ensuring even coverage. Cover or seal and refrigerate for at least an hour, or ideally overnight.

1. Preheat the Oven: Preheat your oven to 375°F (190°C). Grease a baking sheet with cooking spray or a light coating of oil.

2. Bake the Tofu: Arrange the marinated tofu on the prepared baking sheet. Bake for approximately 25-30 minutes, turning the tofu halfway through, until it's firm and slightly golden.

1. Serve: Once baked, remove the tofu from the oven and place it on a serving platter. Garnish with fresh cilantro or green onions if desired.

1. Enjoy: Serve the Baked Coffee-Marinated Tofu as a standalone dish, or use it as a versatile protein option in salads, bowls, wraps, or other plant-based creations.

Achieving a Harmonious Blend of Flavors

Balancing Flavors: The key to successful Coffee-Marinated Tofu is achieving balance. The coffee should be prominent but not overwhelming, allowing other flavors to shine.

Texture Contrast: The robust tofu texture provides an ideal contrast to the coffee's boldness. The tofu's absorbent nature ensures that every bite carries the coffee's aromatic essence.

Taste Testing: Before cooking, taste a small piece of the marinated tofu to gauge the flavor balance. Adjust seasonings as needed to achieve the desired profile.

Cooking Techniques: Pan-Frying and Baking

Pan-Frying Method: Heat a non-stick skillet over medium-high heat. Add a touch of oil and carefully place the marinated tofu in the skillet. Cook until each side is golden brown and crispy, about 3-4 minutes per side. The exterior's crispness contrasts wonderfully with the tender interior.

Baking Method: Preheat your oven to 375°F (190°C). Place the marinated tofu on a parchment-lined baking sheet. Bake for approximately 25-30 minutes, turning the tofu halfway through. Baking produces a firmer texture and a slightly different flavor profile.

Versatility in Plant-Based Delight

With the knowledge of infusing tofu with coffee essence, achieving a harmonious blend of flavors, and mastering the pan-frying and baking techniques, you're poised to create a plant-based masterpiece that captivates both the taste buds and the imagination. Coffee-Marinated Tofu transforms a simple protein source into a canvas for innovation, reflecting the adaptability and creativity inherent in Vietnamese coffee culture. Whether served as a main dish, added to salads, or tucked into sandwiches, this coffee-infused tofu promises a versatile and satisfying culinary adventure.

Chapter 10: Coffee in Baked Goods: Cakes and Cookies

Prepare to embark on a journey that marries the captivating allure of Vietnamese coffee with the delectable realm of baked goods. In this chapter, we'll delve deep into the art of infusing the rich and nuanced flavors of coffee into cakes and cookies, crafting desserts that capture the essence of both tradition and innovation. Uncover the secrets of adding coffee flavor, perfecting coffee concentration in batters, and navigating the intricate dance of baking temperatures and times. Armed with these insights, you'll be equipped to create confections that transcend the ordinary and embody the heart of Vietnamese coffee culture.

Adding Coffee Flavor to Cakes and Cookies

Brewing the Essence: Begin your journey by brewing a robust cup of Vietnamese coffee, allowing its aromas to permeate your senses. This coffee essence will be the cornerstone of your coffee-infused baked creations.

Balancing the Notes: As you incorporate coffee flavor into your baked goods, consider the interplay between the coffee's bold bitterness and the sweetness of your treats. Strive for a harmonious balance that elevates each flavor element.

Synergy of Ingredients: Elevate the coffee essence by pairing it with complementary ingredients. The warmth of vanilla extract, the richness of chocolate, or the depth of warm spices like cinnamon and nutmeg can amplify the coffee's character.

Strengthening the Profile: If you're aiming for a more pronounced coffee flavor, consider experimenting with different coffee brewing methods or exploring unique coffee bean varieties that resonate with your palate.

Determining Coffee Concentration in Batters

Art of Gradual Incorporation: The journey to achieving the perfect coffee concentration in your batters requires experimentation. Start conservatively and gradually increase the coffee essence until you reach the desired intensity.

Taste and Adjust: As you incorporate the coffee essence, remember to taste your batter along the way. Your palate is your guide – adjust the coffee concentration until it resonates harmoniously with the other flavors.

Maintaining Consistency: Keep a watchful eye on the batter's texture. The additional liquid from the coffee essence might necessitate slight adjustments to other wet and dry ingredients to maintain the desired batter consistency.

Baking Temperatures and Times

Coffee's Influence on Baking: Coffee's acidity and moisture content can impact baking temperatures and times. This requires a delicate balance to ensure your baked goods emerge perfectly.

Managing Browning: Due to the acidity in coffee, consider slightly lowering the baking temperature to prevent excessive browning. This gentle adjustment preserves the delightful contrast between the coffee's complex flavors and the golden exterior of your treats.

Testing for Perfection: To ascertain your baked goods' readiness, employ time-tested methods. A toothpick inserted into the center should emerge clean, or your creation should exhibit a luscious golden brown hue.

The Finishing Touch: Once your creations are baked to perfection, embrace the anticipation of the cooling period. Allow your cakes and cookies to rest, as this gentle interlude allows flavors to meld and textures to set.

An Ode to Culinary Fusion

With an in-depth understanding of infusing coffee flavor into baked goods, perfecting coffee concentration in batters, and deftly navigating baking temperatures and times, you're poised to embark on a culinary journey that celebrates the symbiosis of coffee and dessert. From tender coffee-laced cookies that melt in your mouth to intricately layered cakes that unfold with every bite, your creations are poised to encapsulate the essence of Vietnamese coffee culture. As you savor these masterpieces, you'll not only delight your taste buds but also pay homage to the artistry of combining tradition and innovation in the realm of gastronomy.

Chapter 11: Coffee Ice Cream with a Vietnamese Twist

Embark on a frozen journey that marries the captivating allure of Vietnamese coffee with the cool indulgence of ice cream. In this chapter, we'll delve into the art of crafting Coffee Ice Cream with a Vietnamese Twist, a dessert that encapsulates the richness of coffee and the soul of Vietnamese culinary tradition. Discover the secrets of making creamy coffee-infused ice cream, masterfully incorporating Vietnamese ingredients, and serving your creation with a harmonious array of complementary toppings. Prepare to savor the perfect marriage of tradition and innovation, all in a delightful frozen treat.

Making Creamy Coffee-Infused Ice Cream

Choosing the Coffee: Opt for a high-quality Vietnamese coffee that resonates with your palate. The coffee's robustness will infuse the ice cream with depth and character.

Coffee Extraction: Brew a strong cup of Vietnamese coffee, let it cool, and strain it to create a concentrated coffee essence that will form the heart of your ice cream.

Base Ingredients: Prepare a creamy ice cream base using ingredients like heavy cream, milk, sugar, and egg yolks. This velvety base will provide the perfect canvas for your coffee infusion.

Incorporating the Coffee: Gently fold the cooled coffee essence into your ice cream base, balancing the coffee concentration to achieve the desired flavor profile.

Incorporating Vietnamese Ingredients

Sweetened Condensed Milk Magic: Embrace the Vietnamese twist by adding sweetened condensed milk to the ice cream base. This ingredient imparts not only creaminess but also a nostalgic touch of Vietnamese culinary heritage.

Infusing with Spices: Elevate the flavor with Vietnamese spices like cardamom or star anise. These subtle additions lend complexity and a unique twist to your ice cream.

Creating Depth: To intensify the Vietnamese twist, consider adding a drizzle of robust Vietnamese coffee syrup to create a mesmerizing swirl within the ice cream.

Serving Ice Cream with Complementary Toppings

Crunchy Contrasts: Enhance your ice cream experience by incorporating textural contrasts. Consider topping your ice cream with crushed toasted nuts or crispy rice for delightful crunch.

Fruit Elegance: Vietnamese fruits like jackfruit, longan, or lychee complement the coffee-infused ice cream beautifully. The sweet-tart flavors provide a refreshing counterpoint.

Herbal Infusion: Garnish your ice cream with fresh mint or basil leaves. The herbs' aromatic qualities play harmoniously against the rich coffee notes.

Recipes: Vietnamese Coffee Ice Cream & Coffee Syrup
Vietnamese Coffee Ice Cream
Ingredients:

- 2 cups heavy cream
- 1 cup whole milk
- 3/4 cup granulated sugar
- 4 large egg yolks
- 1/4 cup brewed Vietnamese coffee, cooled
- 1/4 cup sweetened condensed milk
- Optional: 1/2 teaspoon cardamom or star anise (ground or crushed)
- Pinch of salt

Instructions:

1. Prepare the Base: In a saucepan, combine heavy cream, milk, and half of the sugar. Heat gently until the mixture is steaming but not boiling.

1. Whisk Egg Yolks: In a separate bowl, whisk egg yolks and the remaining sugar until the mixture is pale and slightly thickened.

1. Temper the Eggs: Gradually pour a small amount of the heated cream mixture into the egg yolks, whisking constantly to temper the eggs.

1. Combine Mixtures: Pour the tempered egg mixture back into the saucepan with the remaining cream mixture. Cook over low heat, stirring constantly, until the mixture thickens and coats the back of a spoon.

1. Add Coffee and Condensed Milk: Remove from heat and stir in the brewed Vietnamese coffee, sweetened condensed milk, optional spices, and salt.

1. Cool and Chill: Strain the mixture to remove any solids. Allow the mixture to cool, then cover and refrigerate for several hours or overnight.

1. Churn and Freeze: Churn the chilled mixture in an ice cream maker according to the manufacturer's instructions. Transfer the churned ice cream to a container and freeze until firm.

Coffee Syrup
Ingredients:

- 1/2 cup brewed Vietnamese coffee
- 1/4 cup granulated sugar

Instructions:

1. Brew Coffee: Prepare a strong cup of Vietnamese coffee.

1. Create Syrup: In a saucepan, combine the brewed coffee and sugar. Heat over medium heat, stirring until the sugar dissolves and the mixture thickens slightly.

1. Cool: Remove from heat and let the syrup cool. Once cooled, transfer it to a container and refrigerate until ready to use.

A Symphony of Sensations

Armed with the knowledge of crafting creamy coffee-infused ice cream, infusing Vietnamese ingredients, and selecting complementary toppings, you're poised to create a culinary masterpiece that embodies the essence of Vietnamese coffee culture. Your Coffee Ice Cream with a Vietnamese Twist captures the heart and soul of tradition while embracing the excitement of innovation. As you take your first spoonful, you'll be transported to the streets of Vietnam, where the aroma of rich coffee and the joy of culinary exploration intertwine in a symphony of sensational flavors.

Chapter 12: Coffee and Sea Salt Body Scrub

Embark on a journey beyond the kitchen as we explore the beauty of Vietnamese coffee in the form of a luxurious Coffee and Sea Salt Body Scrub. In this chapter, we'll delve into the art of crafting exfoliating scrubs that combine the invigorating power of coffee grounds with skin-nourishing ingredients. Discover the secrets of creating a sensory experience that promotes skin health, and uncover the myriad benefits that coffee scrubs bring to your skincare routine. Elevate your self-care regimen with the natural wonders of Vietnamese coffee.

Crafting Coffee-Based Exfoliating Scrubs

Harnessing Coffee's Grit: Coffee grounds, with their coarse texture, serve as excellent natural exfoliants. Their granular nature gently removes dead skin cells, revealing the radiant complexion beneath.

Balancing Exfoliation: Combine coffee grounds with a base ingredient like sea salt, sugar, or Himalayan salt. The salt further aids in exfoliation, allowing for a balanced yet effective scrub.

Embrace Aromatherapy: Enhance the sensory experience by incorporating essential oils like lavender, vanilla, or citrus. The aroma not only uplifts the spirit but also complements the coffee's invigorating scent.

Combining Coffee Grounds with Skin-Nourishing Ingredients

Coconut Oil Elixir: Incorporate skin-loving ingredients like coconut oil, which not only moisturizes but also imparts a silky texture to the scrub.

Vitamin E Infusion: Adding vitamin E oil contributes to skin repair and hydration, leaving the skin feeling supple and rejuvenated.

Antioxidant Boost: Integrate a touch of ground cinnamon or turmeric to enhance the scrub's antioxidant properties, protecting the skin from environmental stressors.

Benefits of Coffee Scrubs for Skin Health

Exfoliation: Coffee scrubs gently slough away dead skin cells, promoting smoother, more radiant skin.

Blood Circulation: The massaging action of using a coffee scrub enhances blood circulation, contributing to a healthy glow.

Reducing Cellulite: Caffeine's natural ability to constrict blood vessels can temporarily reduce the appearance of cellulite.

Anti-Inflammatory Properties: Coffee's antioxidants possess anti-inflammatory properties that can soothe irritated skin.

Awakening the Senses: The invigorating scent of coffee awakens the senses, energizing both the mind and body.

Recipes: Coffee and Sea Salt Body Scrub
Coffee and Sea Salt Body Scrub
Ingredients:

- 1/2 cup coffee grounds (used or unused)
- 1/2 cup sea salt or Epsom salt
- 1/4 cup coconut oil, melted
- 1 teaspoon vitamin E oil
- Optional: 5-10 drops of essential oil (e.g., lavender, citrus, vanilla)

Instructions:

1. Mix Dry Ingredients: In a bowl, combine the coffee grounds and sea salt. Mix well to evenly distribute the exfoliants.

1. Add Oils: Slowly pour in the melted coconut oil and vitamin E oil. Stir to form a cohesive mixture.

1. Incorporate Essential Oil: If desired, add a few drops of your chosen essential oil for an aromatic touch.

1. Store: Transfer the scrub to an airtight container. Ensure that the container is moisture-free to prevent spoilage.

1. Application: In the shower, apply a small amount of the scrub to damp skin. Gently massage in circular motions, paying attention to rough areas.

1. Rinse: Rinse thoroughly with warm water. Pat your skin dry, and feel the newfound softness and radiance.

Embrace the Beauty of Coffee

With the knowledge of crafting coffee-based exfoliating scrubs, combining coffee grounds with skin-nourishing ingredients, and understanding the benefits coffee scrubs offer for skin health, you're ready to embrace the beauty of Vietnamese coffee beyond the cup. Your Coffee and Sea Salt Body Scrub invites you to indulge in a revitalizing experience that pampers your skin and refreshes your senses. As you nurture your skin with the natural wonders of coffee, you'll not only cultivate radiance but also foster a connection between self-care and the cherished traditions of Vietnamese culture.

Chapter 13: Coffee-Infused Cocktails: From Martinis to Old Fashioned

Indulge in a sophisticated blend of flavors as we explore the captivating world of Coffee-Infused Cocktails. In this chapter, we'll delve into the art of elevating classic cocktails with the rich and nuanced essence of Vietnamese coffee. Discover the secrets of crafting cocktails that range from Martinis to Old Fashioned, embracing the synergy between coffee and spirits. Master the mixing techniques that create harmonious and flavorful blends, and explore the art of presentation and garnishing to create memorable sensory experiences that delight the palate and awaken the senses.

Elevating Cocktails with Coffee-Infused Spirits

Creating Coffee-Infused Spirits: Begin your cocktail journey by infusing your favorite spirits, such as vodka, bourbon, or rum, with the flavors of Vietnamese coffee. Allow the coffee's depth to meld seamlessly with the spirit's character.

Coffee Concentration: Experiment with the coffee-to-spirit ratio to achieve the desired coffee intensity. The infusion period can range from a few hours to several days, depending on your preference.

Balancing Ingredients: Consider the spirit's inherent flavors and characteristics when selecting complementary ingredients. The goal is to create a harmonious marriage of flavors that tantalize the taste buds.

Mixing Techniques for Flavorful Blends

The Art of Layering: Embrace the layering technique to create visually stunning cocktails. Layer coffee-infused spirits with liqueurs and other mixers for a mesmerizing effect.

Shaking and Stirring: For cocktails that require mixing, such as Martinis or Espresso Martinis, master the art of shaking or stirring to achieve the ideal dilution and temperature.

Balancing Sweetness and Bitterness: Coffee's inherent bitterness can be balanced with sweet ingredients like syrups, liqueurs, or fresh fruit juices.

Presentation and Garnishing

Visual Elegance: Elevate the cocktail experience with impeccable presentation. Choose glassware that complements the cocktail's color and aesthetic.

Garnishing Finesse: Garnishes are the finishing touch that adds both visual appeal and aromatic complexity. Think coffee beans, citrus twists, or even a dusting of cocoa powder.

Creative Rimming: Experiment with rimming techniques using ingredients like coffee grounds, cocoa powder, or even finely grated chocolate for an added layer of flavor and texture.

Recipes: Coffee-Infused Martini & Vietnamese Coffee Old Fashioned

Coffee-Infused Martini

Ingredients:

- 2 oz coffee-infused vodka
- 1 oz coffee liqueur
- 1/2 oz simple syrup
- Ice
- Coffee beans, for garnish

Instructions:

1. Mix Ingredients: In a shaker, combine the coffee-infused vodka, coffee liqueur, and simple syrup.

1. Shake: Add ice to the shaker and shake vigorously until well-chilled.

1. Strain: Strain the cocktail into a chilled martini glass.

1. Garnish: Float a few coffee beans on the surface for an aromatic finish.

Vietnamese Coffee Old Fashioned
Ingredients:

- 2 oz coffee-infused bourbon
- 1/2 oz simple syrup
- 2-3 dashes of aromatic bitters
- Orange twist, for garnish

Instructions:

1. Muddle and Mix: In a mixing glass, muddle the simple syrup and bitters. Add the coffee-infused bourbon and ice.

1. Stir: Stir the mixture gently to combine and chill.

1. Strain: Strain the cocktail into a rocks glass over a large ice cube.

1. Garnish: Express the oils from an orange twist over the glass, then garnish with the twist.

Elevate the Cocktail Experience

Armed with the knowledge of elevating cocktails with coffee-infused spirits, mastering mixing techniques, and embracing presentation and garnishing finesse, you're poised to elevate your cocktail repertoire to new heights. From the sophisticated allure of a Coffee-Infused Martini to the timeless elegance of a Vietnamese Coffee Old Fashioned, your creations will captivate guests and spark conversations. As you sip these masterfully crafted cocktails, you'll not only enjoy their flavors but also celebrate the fusion of innovation and tradition that defines the world of Vietnamese coffee-infused mixology.

Chapter 14: Vietnamese Coffee Liqueur (Rượu Cà Phê)

Embark on a journey into the realm of liquid luxury as we explore the exquisite world of Vietnamese Coffee Liqueur. In this chapter, we'll delve into the art of crafting this velvety elixir that captures the essence of Vietnamese coffee. Discover the secrets of blending coffee's rich depths with the indulgence of spirits, and unlock the nuances of selecting the right alcohol base. From the creative process of bottling to the finesse of storing, you'll learn to create a homemade Vietnamese Coffee Liqueur that not only enchants the senses but also embodies the heart of this beloved cultural tradition.

Crafting Homemade Coffee Liqueur

The Essence of Vietnamese Coffee: Begin by selecting premium Vietnamese coffee beans that resonate with your palate. The quality of the coffee is paramount to the success of your liqueur.

Balancing Sweetness: Create a rich coffee concentrate and sweeten it with sugar or a simple syrup to achieve the desired level of sweetness. Strike a balance that complements the coffee's complexity.

Infusing Spirits: Infuse your coffee concentrate with a quality spirit like vodka or rum. The spirit serves as a canvas that captures and harmonizes the coffee's depth.

Bottling and Storing Your Creation

Bottling Finesse: Transfer your coffee liqueur to clean, airtight glass bottles. Ensure the bottles are impeccably clean to prevent any contamination.

Aesthetic Appeal: Consider adding a label or tag that not only identifies the liqueur but also reflects the essence of Vietnamese coffee culture.

Storing Wisdom: Store your Vietnamese Coffee Liqueur in a cool, dark place away from direct sunlight. Proper storage preserves the liqueur's flavors and integrity.

Recipe: Vietnamese Coffee Liqueur (Rượu Cà Phê)
Ingredients:

- 1 cup strong Vietnamese coffee, brewed and cooled
- 1 cup vodka or rum
- 3/4 cup granulated sugar
- 1 vanilla bean, split (optional)
- 1 cinnamon stick (optional)

Instructions:

1. Prepare the Coffee: Brew a strong cup of Vietnamese coffee and let it cool.

1. Create the Coffee Concentrate: In a saucepan, combine the brewed coffee and sugar. Heat over medium-low heat until the sugar dissolves and the mixture thickens slightly. Remove from heat and let it cool.

1. Infuse the Spirit: In a clean glass container, combine the coffee concentrate and your chosen alcohol base (vodka or rum). If desired, add the split vanilla bean and cinnamon stick.

1. Seal and Rest: Seal the container tightly and let the mixture infuse for at least 2 weeks, shaking it gently every few days to encourage the flavors to meld.

1. Strain and Bottle: After the infusion period, strain the mixture through a fine mesh strainer to remove any coffee grounds or solids. Transfer the liqueur to clean glass bottles.

1. Serve and Savor: Your homemade Vietnamese Coffee Liqueur is ready to enjoy! Sip it neat, on the rocks, or use it as a delightful ingredient in various cocktails and desserts.

Crafted Elegance in a Bottle

With the knowledge of crafting homemade coffee liqueur, selecting the right alcohol base, and mastering the art of bottling and storing, you're poised to create a liquid masterpiece that encapsulates the allure of Vietnamese coffee culture. Your Vietnamese Coffee Liqueur is a testament to the artistry of blending tradition and innovation, and it invites you to savor the depths of coffee in an entirely new and enchanting form. As you sip this velvety elixir, you'll be transported to the heart of Vietnam, where the rich aroma of coffee intertwines with the warmth of hospitality.

Chapter 15: Coffee-Inspired Smoothie Bowls

Embark on a journey of wholesome indulgence as we explore the harmonious fusion of coffee and nutrient-packed bowls in Coffee-Inspired Smoothie Bowls. In this chapter, we'll delve into the art of crafting vibrant smoothie bowls that seamlessly incorporate the captivating essence of Vietnamese coffee. Discover the secrets of balancing coffee flavor with an array of fruits and toppings, and embrace the creativity of preparing smoothie bowl artistry that awakens your senses and nourishes your body. With this chapter as your guide, you'll be empowered to create smoothie bowls that reflect the essence of Vietnamese coffee culture while promoting well-being.

Incorporating Coffee into Nutrient-Packed Bowls

Coffee Elixir: Begin your journey by brewing a strong cup of Vietnamese coffee. This coffee elixir will infuse your smoothie bowl with a depth of flavor that resonates on multiple levels.

The Power of Base Ingredients: Build the foundation of your smoothie bowl with nutrient-rich ingredients like banana, avocado, Greek yogurt, or nut milk. These bases provide creaminess and essential nutrients.

Boosting Nutritional Value: Enhance the nutritional value by adding superfoods like chia seeds, flax seeds, spinach, or spirulina. These ingredients elevate the bowl's health benefits.

Balancing Coffee Flavor with Fruit and Toppings

Fruit Harmony: Select a variety of fruits that harmonize with coffee's complexity. Ripe bananas, berries, and tropical fruits like mango complement the coffee flavor beautifully.

Texture and Crunch: Incorporate a mix of textures by adding crunchy elements such as granola, nuts, and seeds. These layers of texture enhance the overall sensory experience.

Sweetness and Variety: Sweeten your smoothie bowl with natural sweeteners like honey, maple syrup, or agave nectar. Experiment with the balance of sweetness to create a harmonious profile.

Preparing Smoothie Bowl Artistry

Layering Aesthetics: Embrace the art of layering to create visually captivating smoothie bowls. Alternate between coffee-infused and fruit-based layers for a striking effect.

Garnish Elegance: Elevate your smoothie bowl's presentation with an array of artistic garnishes. Think coffee beans, coconut flakes, edible flowers, or drizzles of honey.

Symphony of Colors: Play with a spectrum of colors by incorporating different fruits and toppings. The visual vibrancy of your smoothie bowl will be a feast for the eyes.

Recipes: Coffee-Infused Banana Smoothie Bowl & Berry Coffee Delight Bowl
Coffee-Infused Banana Smoothie Bowl
Ingredients:

- 1 ripe banana, frozen
- 1/2 cup brewed Vietnamese coffee, cooled
- 1/2 cup Greek yogurt or plant-based yogurt
- 1 tablespoon almond butter
- 1 tablespoon chia seeds
- Optional: 1 teaspoon honey or maple syrup
- Toppings: Sliced banana, granola, chopped nuts, drizzle of honey

Instructions:

1. Blend Ingredients: In a blender, combine the frozen banana, brewed coffee, Greek yogurt, almond butter, chia seeds, and optional sweetener. Blend until smooth.

1. Assemble: Pour the smoothie into a bowl. Arrange the sliced banana, granola, and chopped nuts on top.

1. Drizzle: Finish with a drizzle of honey or your preferred sweetener.

Berry Coffee Delight Bowl
Ingredients:

- 1 cup mixed berries (strawberries, blueberries, raspberries)
- 1/2 cup brewed Vietnamese coffee, cooled
- 1/2 cup coconut water or almond milk

- 1/4 cup rolled oats
- 1 tablespoon flax seeds
- Toppings: Fresh berries, shredded coconut, chia seeds

Instructions:

1. Blend Ingredients: In a blender, combine the mixed berries, brewed coffee, coconut water or almond milk, rolled oats, and flax seeds. Blend until creamy.

1. Pour and Decorate: Pour the berry-coffee blend into a bowl. Top with fresh berries, shredded coconut, and chia seeds.

Embrace the Art of Nourishment

With the knowledge of incorporating coffee into nutrient-packed bowls, balancing coffee flavor with an array of fruits and toppings, and preparing smoothie bowl artistry, you're ready to embark on a culinary journey that nourishes both body and soul. Your Coffee-Inspired Smoothie Bowls encapsulate the essence of Vietnamese coffee culture while celebrating the vibrant colors and flavors of nature. As you savor each spoonful, you'll experience the joy of crafting a nutritious masterpiece that fuels your day with energy and delight.

Chapter 16: Savory Dishes: Coffee-Rubbed Ribs

Embark on a journey of culinary fusion as we explore the exquisite marriage of coffee and savory dishes with Coffee-Rubbed Ribs. In this chapter, we'll delve into the art of applying coffee rubs to create tender and flavorful ribs that capture the essence of Vietnamese coffee culture. Discover the secrets of slow cooking and grilling techniques that elevate your ribs to delectable perfection, and explore the art of pairing them with complementary accompaniments. From the aromatic rub to the succulent meat, your Coffee-Rubbed Ribs will become a culinary masterpiece that celebrates the symphony of flavors.

Applying Coffee Rubs to Savory Ribs

Creating the Coffee Rub: Begin by crafting a balanced coffee rub that complements the richness of the ribs. Combine finely ground Vietnamese coffee with a blend of spices that enhance the coffee's depth.

Flavorful Complexity: Experiment with a mix of spices such as smoked paprika, brown sugar, garlic powder, cayenne pepper, and a pinch of salt. These ingredients will create a nuanced flavor profile.

Rubbing Technique: Gently massage the coffee rub onto the ribs, ensuring an even coating. Allow the ribs to marinate and absorb the flavors for a few hours or overnight.

Slow Cooking and Grilling Techniques

Low and Slow: Slow cooking is a hallmark of achieving tender ribs. Start by baking or roasting the rubbed ribs at a low temperature to allow the flavors to meld and the meat to become fork-tender.

Grilling Charisma: Finish your ribs on the grill to impart a tantalizing smoky flavor and a beautiful charred crust. Baste the ribs with a coffee-infused glaze during the grilling process for an added layer of flavor.

Temperature Mastery: Monitor the internal temperature of the ribs during both slow cooking and grilling to ensure they reach the perfect level of tenderness without becoming overcooked.

Pairing with Accompaniments

Balancing Act: The richness of Coffee-Rubbed Ribs can be balanced with vibrant accompaniments. Consider serving your ribs with a fresh salad, slaw, or pickled vegetables.

Savory Sides: Incorporate savory sides like garlic mashed potatoes, roasted vegetables, or a medley of grilled corn and bell peppers to complement the flavor profile.

Dipping Delights: Offer a selection of dipping sauces that enhance the ribs' taste. Tangy barbecue sauce, spicy sriracha mayo, or a zesty chimichurri can elevate the dining experience.

Coffee glaze (as prepared)

- Salt and black pepper, to taste

Instructions:

Prepare the Coffee Rub: In a bowl, combine all the coffee rub ingredients. Mix well to create a uniform rub.

Rub the Ribs: Pat the ribs dry and generously coat them with the coffee rub. Massage the rub into the meat to ensure even coverage. Refrigerate for at least 2 hours or overnight.

Slow Cook the Ribs: Preheat the oven to 250°F (120°C). Place the rubbed ribs on a baking sheet or in a roasting pan. Slow cook the ribs for about 2.5 to 3 hours, until the meat is tender.

Prepare the Coffee Glaze: In a saucepan, combine all the coffee glaze ingredients. Simmer over low heat until the glaze thickens slightly. Set aside.

Grill the Ribs: Preheat a grill to medium-high heat. Brush the slow-cooked ribs with the coffee glaze on both sides. Grill the ribs for about 5-7 minutes per side, basting with glaze occasionally, until they develop a caramelized crust.

Serve: Once the ribs are cooked to perfection, remove them from the grill and let them rest for a few minutes. Slice the ribs and serve them with your choice of accompaniments.

A Symphony of Savory Delights

With the knowledge of applying coffee rubs to savory ribs, mastering slow cooking and grilling techniques, and embracing the art of pairing with complementary accompaniments, you're poised to create a symphony of flavors that elevate your dining experience. Your Coffee-Rubbed Ribs with Coffee Glaze capture the essence of Vietnamese coffee culture while infusing every bite with a depth of taste that tantalizes the palate. As you savor the succulent meat and aromatic nuances, you'll be reminded of the intricate dance between tradition and innovation that defines the culinary landscape.

Chapter 17: Coffee-Infused Chocolate Truffles

Embark on a journey of indulgence as we explore the exquisite combination of coffee and chocolate in the form of decadent Coffee-Infused Chocolate Truffles. In this chapter, we'll delve into the art of merging the rich, robust flavors of Vietnamese coffee with velvety chocolate to create truffles that redefine luxury. Discover the secrets of crafting ganache with coffee undertones, mastering the art of rolling and coating truffles creatively, and presenting these morsels of delight that embody the essence of Vietnamese coffee culture.

Merging Coffee and Chocolate in Decadent Truffles

A Match Made in Heaven: Coffee and chocolate share a harmonious relationship that amplifies the richness of both flavors. The earthiness of coffee complements the sweetness of chocolate.

Flavor Spectrum: Experiment with different types of chocolate, from dark to milk to white, to achieve the desired balance of flavors.

Texture Variation: Incorporate texture by adding crushed nuts, cocoa nibs, or cookie crumbs to the truffle mixture. These elements enhance the sensory experience.

Creating Ganache with Coffee Undertones

Preparing Ganache: Craft a luscious ganache by combining high-quality chocolate with heavy cream. This velvety mixture forms the heart of your truffles.

Infusing Coffee: Brew a strong cup of Vietnamese coffee and let it cool. Gently fold the coffee into the ganache to infuse it with a depth of flavor.

Balancing Creaminess: Achieve the perfect balance between the coffee's intensity and the ganache's creaminess. Taste and adjust as needed.

Rolling and Coating Truffles Creatively

Shaping the Truffles: Once the ganache is set, use a spoon or a melon baller to scoop out portions. Roll the ganache between your palms to form small, uniform balls.

Coating Magic: Dip the truffle balls in melted chocolate or cocoa powder, rolling them until fully coated. This step adds an extra layer of chocolate and visual appeal.

Creative Finishes: Experiment with coatings like crushed coffee beans, shredded coconut, or finely chopped nuts. These embellishments contribute to the truffles' charm.

Recipe: Coffee-Infused Dark Chocolate Truffles
Coffee-Infused Dark Chocolate Truffles
Ingredients:

- 8 oz high-quality dark chocolate, finely chopped
- 1/2 cup heavy cream
- 1/4 cup strong brewed Vietnamese coffee, cooled
- 1 tablespoon unsalted butter, softened
- Pinch of salt
- Coating options: Cocoa powder, finely chopped nuts, crushed coffee beans

Instructions:

1. Create Ganache: Place the finely chopped dark chocolate in a heatproof bowl. In a saucepan, heat the heavy cream over medium heat until it's just about to boil. Pour the cream over the chocolate and let it sit for a minute. Gently whisk until smooth.

1. Infuse with Coffee: Add the brewed Vietnamese coffee, softened butter, and a pinch of salt to the ganache. Gently fold the mixture until well combined and silky.

1. Chill and Shape: Cover the bowl with plastic wrap and refrigerate the ganache for about 2 hours or until it's firm enough to handle. Using a spoon or melon baller, scoop out portions of ganache and roll them into small balls between your palms.

1. Coat the Truffles: Roll the ganache balls in your chosen coating option, such as cocoa powder, finely chopped nuts, or crushed coffee beans. Ensure the truffles are fully coated.

1. Chill and Serve: Place the coated truffles on a parchment-lined tray and refrigerate for another 30 minutes to firm up. Once set, your Coffee-Infused Dark Chocolate Truffles are ready to be savored.

A Confectionery Symphony

With the knowledge of merging coffee and chocolate in decadent truffles, creating ganache with coffee undertones, and rolling and coating truffles creatively, you're prepared to embark on a confectionery journey that celebrates the union of flavors and cultures. Your Coffee-Infused Chocolate Truffles reflect the essence of Vietnamese coffee culture while indulging the senses with each sumptuous bite. As you present these edible jewels to your loved ones or guests, you'll be inviting them to savor a symphony of flavors that encapsulate the magic of coffee and chocolate in perfect harmony.

Chapter 18: Iced Matcha Coffee (Cà Phê Xanh)

Embark on a journey of fusion as we explore the captivating union of Vietnamese coffee and Matcha Green Tea in Iced Matcha Coffee. In this chapter, we'll delve into the art of marrying the rich and robust flavors of coffee with the earthy and vibrant notes of matcha, creating a harmonious beverage that reflects the essence of both cultures. Discover the secrets of achieving the perfect balance of flavors, and embrace the elegance of whipping up Iced Matcha Coffee that refreshes and delights the senses.

Marrying Vietnamese Coffee with Matcha Green Tea

Cultural Fusion: The marriage of Vietnamese coffee and Matcha Green Tea celebrates the beauty of cultural diversity, merging two beloved beverages into a single masterpiece.

Taste Synergy: Coffee's bold and robust flavors complement matcha's vegetal, earthy notes. Together, they create a layered taste profile that tantalizes the palate.

Texture Harmony: Matcha's velvety texture harmonizes with the creamy mouthfeel of Vietnamese coffee, resulting in a beverage that's both satisfying and refreshing.

Achieving Harmony in Flavor Profiles

Balancing Act: Achieve a harmonious balance between the coffee and matcha flavors. Allow each element to shine without overpowering the other.

Sweetness Consideration: Depending on personal preference, add a touch of sweetness to round out the flavors. Options include condensed milk, simple syrup, or flavored syrups.

Experimentation: Experiment with different coffee-to-matcha ratios to find the perfect balance that resonates with your taste buds.

Whipping Up Iced Matcha Coffee Elegance

Brew Vietnamese Coffee: Begin by brewing a strong cup of Vietnamese coffee and letting it cool. This will be the foundation of your Iced Matcha Coffee.

Prepare Matcha: Whisk Matcha Green Tea powder with water until smooth and frothy. The vibrant green hue will contrast beautifully with the coffee.

Layering Technique: Create layers of flavor by alternating between the brewed Vietnamese coffee and the prepared matcha. This layering technique creates a visually appealing gradient effect.

Recipe: Iced Vietnamese Coffee Matcha Latte
Iced Vietnamese Coffee Matcha Latte
Ingredients:

- 1 cup strong Vietnamese coffee, cooled
- 1 teaspoon Matcha Green Tea powder
- 2 tablespoons hot water
- Sweetener of choice (condensed milk, simple syrup, etc.)
- Ice cubes

Instructions:

1. Prepare Matcha: In a bowl, whisk the Matcha Green Tea powder with hot water until smooth and frothy.

1. Sweeten the Coffee: Sweeten the strong Vietnamese coffee to taste using your preferred sweetener.

1. Assemble the Layers: Fill a glass with ice cubes. Slowly pour the sweetened Vietnamese coffee over the ice, filling the glass about halfway.

1. Add Matcha Layer: Gently pour the prepared Matcha Green Tea over the coffee layer, allowing it to create a second layer on top.

1. Serve: Stir gently to combine the layers. Enjoy your Iced Vietnamese Coffee Matcha Latte immediately.

A Fusion of Refreshment
With the knowledge of marrying Vietnamese coffee with Matcha Green Tea, achieving harmony in flavor profiles, and whipping up Iced Matcha Coffee elegance, you're poised to create a beverage that transcends cultural boundaries and awakens the senses. Your Iced

Vietnamese Coffee Matcha Latte is a testament to the culinary art of fusion, inviting you to savor the intriguing symphony of flavors that blend tradition with innovation. As you take that refreshing sip, you'll be reminded of the ever-evolving culinary landscape that embraces diversity and creativity.

Chapter 19: Coffee Tasting and Pairing Tips

Embark on a journey of sensory exploration as we delve into the world of Coffee Tasting and Pairing. In this chapter, we'll guide you through the art of unraveling the nuances of different coffee beans, understanding coffee flavor profiles and descriptors, and mastering the delicate dance of pairing coffee with an array of foods and desserts. With this chapter as your guide, you'll elevate your appreciation of Vietnamese coffee culture to new heights, discovering the art of savoring and pairing coffee that captivates the senses.

Exploring the Nuances of Different Coffee Beans

Bean Origins: Begin by exploring the diverse origins of coffee beans, from the highlands of Vietnam to other renowned coffee-producing regions around the world.

Single-Origin vs. Blends: Understand the differences between single-origin coffees and blends. Each offers unique flavor profiles derived from their growing conditions.

Tasting Varieties: Sample different coffee bean varieties, such as Arabica and Robusta, to understand their distinct characteristics and how they contribute to the final cup.

Coffee Flavor Profiles and Descriptors

Flavor Wheel: Familiarize yourself with the coffee flavor wheel, a tool that breaks down the various tasting notes and aromas found in coffee. This wheel is an essential guide for identifying flavors.

Aroma Identification: Practice identifying aromas like fruity, nutty, floral, earthy, and chocolatey. These descriptors provide insights into the coffee's complexity.

Taste Mapping: Develop your palate by tasting a variety of coffees and mapping their flavor profiles. Compare different beans to understand the range of flavors.

Pairing Coffee with Food and Desserts

Complementary Pairings: Consider the principles of complementary flavors when pairing coffee with food. For example, pair a bright and citrusy coffee with a zesty dessert.

Contrasting Pairings: Experiment with contrasting pairings, where the coffee's bitterness balances the sweetness of a dessert, creating a harmonious contrast.

Texture and Weight: Pay attention to the texture and weight of both the coffee and the food. Light coffees can pair well with delicate pastries, while robust coffees stand up to richer desserts.

Tips for a Successful Coffee Tasting

Clean Palate: Begin with a clean palate by avoiding strong flavors before the tasting. This ensures that your taste buds can fully appreciate the coffee's nuances.

Small Sips: Take small sips of coffee, allowing it to coat your palate. Swirl the coffee in your mouth to fully experience its flavors.

Note-Taking: Keep a tasting journal to record your observations, including the coffee's aroma, body, acidity, and aftertaste. This practice helps refine your palate.

Crafting Memorable Coffee Experiences

With the knowledge of exploring the nuances of different coffee beans, understanding coffee flavor profiles and descriptors, and mastering the art of pairing coffee with food and desserts, you're prepared to craft memorable coffee experiences that transcend the cup. Your ability to identify and appreciate the subtle complexities of coffee elevates your connection to Vietnamese coffee culture, inviting you to explore the ever-evolving landscape of flavors. As you indulge in the delights of pairing and tasting, you'll unlock a world of sensory pleasure that deepens your understanding of coffee's rich heritage.

As we bring our culinary journey through "Vietnamese Coffee Recipes" to a close, we reflect on the rich tapestry of flavors, aromas, and experiences that this journey has offered. From traditional brews that have stood the test of time to innovative creations that push the boundaries of coffee culture, this cookbook has been a celebration of the vibrant and diverse world of Vietnamese coffee.

We've delved into the art of crafting the perfect cup of Vietnamese drip coffee, explored a spectrum of delightful beverages that infuse coffee with new dimensions, and ventured into the realm of culinary creations where coffee meets cuisine. From sweet to savory, hot to cold, and every sensory delight in between, this cookbook has illuminated the countless ways in which coffee can be a muse for culinary innovation.

Our exploration extended beyond the cup, as we delved into the art of pairing and tasting coffee. Understanding the nuances of different coffee beans, deciphering flavor profiles, and mastering the art of pairing coffee with foods and desserts have enriched our appreciation of the complex symphony of flavors that coffee can offer.

As you embark on your own culinary adventures, we hope that "Vietnamese Coffee Recipes" serves as both a guide and an inspiration. May these recipes and insights not only tantalize your taste buds but also transport you to the vibrant streets of Vietnam, where coffee culture is a way of life. With each sip and bite, may you be reminded of the rich cultural heritage, creativity, and innovation that make up the world of Vietnamese coffee.

So, whether you're sipping on a traditional cà phê sữa đá, indulging in a coffee-infused dessert, or crafting your own unique coffee creation, remember that every cup and dish is an invitation to experience the beauty of coffee culture in all its forms. As you continue to explore and create, may your love for Vietnamese coffee flourish, and may your culinary endeavors be filled with the same passion and delight that have guided us on this remarkable journey.

Cheers to the love of coffee, the joy of creation, and the cultural connections that unite us all. May your culinary adventures continue to awaken your senses and nourish your soul.